Christ Gave Me This Pen

So I Have to Write the Truth

Kim B Miller

All of these copyrighted poems were created by Kim B Miller and they cannot be reproduced, copied, used, or sold in any way, shape or form without the written consent of the author. All rights are reserved.

THE HOLY BIBLE, NEW INTERNATIONAL VERSION®, NIV® Copyright © 1973, 1978, 1984, 2011 by Biblica, Inc. ™ Used by permission. All rights reserved worldwide.

© Copyright 2016 Kim B. Miller.
All Rights Reserved.

Dedication

I'd like to dedicate this book to Christ. Thanks for allowing me to write; thanks for allowing me to see; thanks for opening my mind to your wisdom. I hope I make you proud.

Romans 5:6-8: New International Version (NIV)

[6] You see, at just the right time, when we were still powerless, Christ died for the ungodly. [7] Very rarely will anyone die for a righteous person, though for a good person someone might possibly dare to die. [8] But God demonstrates his own love for us in this: While we were still sinners, Christ died for us.

Table of Contents

Name	Page
1. The Light	1
2. He is Waiting	5
3. Pain	11
4. He is	15
5. Assassin	19
6. Lost	23
7. Line	27
8. Flawed	33
9. Temple	37
10. Reality	43
11. Duality	47
12. Not Jesus	51
13. The Word	55
14. Praise	59
15. Sin-cere	63
16. Here	67
17. Christian Truths	71
18. I'm Sorry	75
19. Forgive	79
20. Love	83
Haiku	87
Kimism	93
Notes	115

Light

2 Samuel 23:4
He is like the light of morning at sunrise on a cloudless morning, like the brightness after rain that brings grass from the earth.

He is the light that restores peace to a once restless heart
Radiantly feeding us hope
Like Lot's wife we look back
Leaning on the Lord but tilted toward the world
Jesus is the light that illuminates our souls
Yet we install dimmers
Darkness bleeding in
Scrubbed our soul free of relevance
Trying to be disciples to He, who we have not yet served
While we fixate on me, myself and I
The true Trinity gets ignored
We have our baggage hidden, neatly folded and put away so others can't see it
Don't put your baggage in God's closet
Fighting only for causes you believe in
Blinded by the lust for things that limit your growth

The path to Heaven is paved by those who gave, not those who took
Singing I surrender all
When only part of the white flag waves
Throwing crumbs at God's table disguised at meals
Look at the mirror
Serving two masters is serving yourself
You can't manufacture the soul filled quietness that comes from God
Real light will illuminate the flaws in your artificial glow
The army of the Lord is not just strong in number
Their vigilance of the Word is unshakable
So bring your incomplete officers to the field
Truth will win
God will rule
And mercy will fill this land
For the Lord works with all who call on Him
Now stand it the shelter His presence provides
The choice is yours
You are not waiting for Him
He is waiting for you
He is not the cross you put on
He is the words you speak

Out of the heart the tongue flows
If you don't like what's coming out
Focus on what you're letting in

 # He is Waiting

Here we are children of a King
A loving, merciful Father
Who thought enough of us to send the Author and
Finisher of our Faith
To atone not for Himself but for all we've done
Unselfishly punished for sins we revealed in
Beaten, ridiculed and tortured
He gave His life
Where were we
We were under His body avoiding every blow
Though we caused the fight
We were on the sidelines throwing stones
Though we told the lies
We were shouting defiantly I know you not
Though we pointed Him out
Blaming one for treachery
Yet we all should be on trial
Judas couldn't see Jesus for the 30 pieces of silver
What's blocking your view
Why does the creator have to wait for you to
recognize his gifts
You thank everyone but Him
Yet He is waiting

The sun is bright and healing the darkness that once embraced you
You thanked the sky when the sun soaked radiance upon your skin
Yet He is waiting
You gather your strength to face a day filled with doubts
Slowly excavating the light God gave you
You let glimmers of brightness escape
Saturation avoided
Holding back your light for an audience you deem worthy
Yet He is waiting
Consuming negativity to link to others
You chameleon yourself to assimilate
Rather than letting the lesson be taught through you
Integrating hatred to become liked
Joining the poison, more lethal, more potent
Instead of letting the love spring forth
You become woven into the world
Yet He is waiting
Absorbing lessons provided by teachers entrenched in their own words

Untrained ears drinking ignorance

Awareness available yet we look away

Focused on fiction while truth waits to be discovered

Bible ready for learning but Christmas or Easter is not upon us

So usage is overlooked

Yet He is waiting

We say here I am Lord

Praying another disciple gets anointed

So we can Amen from the sidelines

Yet He is waiting

Quoting verses as long as they are not in the Bible

Repeating earthly affirmations

There is no Book of Star Wars, Scandal or NFL

Yet some focus more on these then their own salvation

Looking toward temporary fixes

While permanent peace waits to be recognized

Yet He is waiting

Worried about earthly judgment

While your soul drifts aimlessly without purpose

Trying to serve two masters

Neither of them God

Yet He is waiting

You are desperately anchored to pride

While the inventor of love waits for it to be sent back to Him

Jesus is calling

He is the answer

Put your pride down and pick your Bible up

How much longer does He have to wait

Yet He is waiting

Pain

I see you

I see you struggling

I see you wondering why you

You are not the problem

You are beautiful

You only see your beauty when the shine shines

I see it when it rains

Pain is not your friend but she is a necessary part of each journey

She tries to get rid of your other companions: joy, love and pride

She wants to isolate you

That way you think it's just her and you

Your spirit is your strength

Love is your armor

So the only way to destroy you is to get you to do it

Pain will try to get you to drink poison

She will try to block your vision so your accomplishments are written in chalk

But your disappointments are written in soul ink

Think past her

She doesn't speak for you

But she will consume your wisdom if you don't

Pain doesn't move out

She has to be evicted

She can't leave unless you want her to

She wants you to want her

But she can't have you

He is

Man will talk to you of history
Facts they can, wrap in paper, put on a bow and present to you as truth
But the unseen cannot be explained
A God that created all we imagine is dismissed
Human arrogance takes His place
Their limited vision can't see Greatness
Echoing what God is not
Claiming God's blessings, while crediting themselves
Trying to put earthly bows on Heavenly treasures
They can hide in the darkness but we live in His light
A light so brilliant even darkness cannot contain it
We act like Christians
Pretending to be Holy
Don't play pretend with God
There is no Academy Award for Christians
If you think you can put God on a shelf
You don't know who you serve
If someone can make you put your religion down, it was never up
You are either with God or you're not
Be a Christian, get off the fence
There are no fences in Heaven

Pick a side
You either hot or cold
He's looking for someone who is willing to live His Word
When we fall we don't head for the shelf we head toward our Savior
Saved by the One that thought we were worth the journey
No greater love
To come to a fight He didn't start
To save sinners
Mighty the hand but gentle the soul
But we assist in our own ignorance
Ignoring the scripture that guide our steps
We walk off the path into the arms of a world
Where money is more important than heath
Until they're sick
Where prayer should only be done at church
Unless there's a school shooting
We follow the world into a ditch then we look back instead of looking up
The calling of the righteous is just
Follow your path to your Biblical truth

No path is empty, God is there

Sin is temporary but God is forever

Don't focus on the stumbles

Sometimes you fall so you can show somebody else how to get up

Don't hide your struggles

Let them produce the fruit that the Lord is cultivating

2 Corinthians 5:7 - (For we walk by faith, not by sight:)

You don't have to see the path to walk on it

You only have to know who sent you

# Assassin

I'm an assassin
I killed three people today
I have a hollow tip pen and I love using it
My tongue is dripping from your blood
I used my words as a weapon of mass destruction
Targets acquired
The acid that I'm spewing is meant to kill
The knife that slices your throat so severely is not made of metal
There is no blade in my hand
The blade is in my throat
It annunciates your pain
Target neutralized
Neutralized by a couple of words from my tongue meant to sting
No kill
No to decapitate your spirit
You the willing victim
Standing before me with a target painted on your soul
Why do you wait to be killed
Is a bullet what you think you deserve
Is that why you aren't ducking as I shoot hate toward you

Death be calling your name
Where's your Teflon
Where's your hater proof vest and your "shade" resistant armor
I can only assassinate those who inhale my hate
I can only assassinate those who are drinking the poison I served
Some of you only drink poison
So another flavor of arsenic would be a welcome addition to your collection of pain
Don't close your eyes
That won't make the penetration of my words any softer
Look at me
I killed three people today
How many people did you assassinate

Lost

Does the Holy Spirit live in you
Does it sanctify you with truth
Will you allow its guidance
Or will you surpass the very help you claim to want
Will you jump and shout hallelujah
While running toward destruction
You can amen yourself into a coma
And still be distant from God
Running endlessly
Rather than giving God a chance to release your pain
Pain is your confidant
Stroking the ego that you have built
Towering over reality
You only seek her counsel
Just touch the hem of His garment and you shall be healed
Threads hang near but you will not stretch to receive what is yours
Breathing in you wait for a resurrection that has already taken place
Waiting for a personal invitation to glory
Yet another excuse to side step His grace
Pushing ignorance in a stroller like it was you first born

Crutches in hand you blindly walk through life
Foolishness welcomed while wisdom withers in the corner ignored
Scripture erased one word at a time
As you replace it with empty thoughts
Fake soothing waves wash into your heart
Drowning on dry land
Your Savior awaits you
Dismissing Him again you go to wander in the dessert of your mind
The solitude is His
Yet He shares it
His love ignored
Dropping shade on God's Son
Jesus an afterthought for victory
Yet the cause for glory
You walk only because He says so
Yet you use those very steps to walk away from Him
Run away
Walk away
Throw your time to the air
You think you have a plan
God gave you all you need

If you need a plan b God is not your plan a

The race is over, time is up, a few seconds to judgment

This meeting cannot be removed from your calendar

The world seems pointless

What have I done

Time wasted

Walking away from God

Walking away from my eternity

This is what lost looks like

Determined to be free I lost myself

I lost everything

Line

The light is so bright in here, the picture so real

I am walking around "saints" and we all just died and

we are wondering where we are

Looking around unspoken bigotry exposes itself

It can't be Heaven if you're here monkey

A "Brutha" in the back agrees for all the wrong

reasons

Whites ain't allowed in either

The slurs flow freely as I look around searching for a

destination

Slowly the fog lifts as we look upward to a staircase

on a cloud labeled sinners

I run to get in line while others stay in place

Aren't you going

That's not my line

As they stared I wonder why they hesitated

Another stairway appeared and another and another

With titles blazingly: No blacks, no whites, no gays, no straight, no …..

There were lines for hate I never heard of

Every line filled we waited

Slowly the clouds evaporated and the lines became clearer

The once confident haters expressionless as they see their line loops up and then down

Up long enough to hear the wrongness of their path

Up long enough to see light

Up long enough to see their reflection etched in arrogance

Up long enough to see the One that they chose to ignore

The sinner line was full of imperfection

Granted audience not because they were perfect but because they realized they were sinners

Heaven is a place built on love

So ask yourself which staircase you would belong in

Answer not unto me

Answer unto Him

Some of you will say I'm not hateful

Here's what you don't understand

You don't pick your staircase, your staircase picks you

Inner truth supersedes external lies

The judgment book is waiting

Some of you are more worried about Facebook than facing that book

There will be no likes to choose and no comments to make

Those who used endless hours spreading hate

produced their final ending

Judges got judged

Sinners got love

Which staircase would chose you

Flawed

Block my blessings
Kill off my dreams
I've already done that
I've already taught myself misery
So my inability to fly is not because my wings are broken
It's because I won't stretch them out far enough to try
I am flawed but the Lord saw fit to let these wings soar
I was looking for perfect wings
He was looking for someone willing to leave the safety of the nest
Contrary to popular belief we Christians do not stand tall all the time
We get weak
So if your vision is looking for perfection you won't see us
If you want to see a Christian look for someone who is on the ground sobbing but still praising Him
Crawling to victory and still thanking Him
Sick but believing He will provide healing
You see Christians may not always be standing
But we always have help getting up

The world sees shattered pieces of hope
But God can make whole what has been broken
He just can't fight you while putting the pieces back in place
Aren't you the one who broke you
Now the Prince of Peace is putting your pieces together
His only obstacle is you
Rejecting the very help you claim to pray for
Just work with Him
Pick up your cross
Why don't you pick up your cross instead of comparing it to others
Side view mirrors often come with a warning
Crosses that appear in an envious mirror may appear smaller than the actual size
Prayer abbreviated
We only bend down long enough to say thank you and we are already standing up by the time we get to you
We throw seconds at God but look for a lifetime of peace

Peace has to be invited and she doesn't take many invitations because they're not genuine
Drop the robe judge
Your record of my sins don't count
Since you're claiming Jesus' responsibilities let's see if you have any of His abilities
Walk on water, no you'd drown
Heal the sick, no you have a cold
Speak truth, no you use your mouth to spread lies
If I touch the hem of your garment the only thing that happens is my knees get dirty from bending so low
Cricket is not just a game played in England
It wouldn't hurt for some of you to learn to play the American version by shutting your mouth to my sins and concentrating on your own
I'm cleaning my closet
Isn't it time you found your way to yours

Temple

I've decided my body is a temple
My black is beautiful
My curves are perfect
I've decided to look in the mirror and love who is staring back at me
So walk away and take your hate with you
I'm Kim B, B to the 6th power
Black, bold, brilliant, blessed, Brooklynite
For those of you still counting that's five
6 is back off
You can't determine my strength by looking at me
This temple is fortified by God
Love is the foundation
But you only tear down what you don't understand
I know love
So your wrecking ball has no affect here
Your words don't stick
I'm standing strong
I can matrix out of your hate
Unweave your plan of destruction and still thrive
I know you saw me down and thought I was out
But you didn't look close enough
I was down on my knees praying

The lemons you threw
Hoping to overwhelm me
I took your lemons and made cookies, cake, pudding, and pie
Now I'm sipping on lemonade that you provided the ingredients for
While you choke on indecision
Take your judgments and try to find a sponge that is willing to absorb the crap you are spewing
I stopped listening
But if you ever feel the need to try to knock this sister down again
You're going to need a bigger arsenal then what you got
I've being ricocheting haters off since I could walk
This is the A-team
I'm BA Baracus without the jewelry
Tough and resilient
Opportunity does not knock on my door she lives here
You see I made room for her
So whether I'm broken or not my pen still writes
You want to be butterfly without putting in the time to be a caterpillar

You want to sparkle like a gem put you can't polish crap into a stone
You don't get it
Diamonds are not only clear
They come in many colors
But they all start off as black coal
So my blackness is not the problem
It's a gift given to me
To protect me from the brilliance of the light that I will be walking in
I'm not deterred by you
My vision can't be blocked by your shade
I'll take the shade you throw, set up lawn chairs under it and thank God for the seat
You see shade can only be seen in the light
I'm not willing to entertain your disdain on who I used to be
The past is not a reflection on who I am now
All you got is old dirt that the Lord already washed clean
Deep light penetrates all darkness
So wash your mouth clean of my name

I know it taste sweet since I'm all you seem to talk about
I know you're looking for hate to win
But I already told you
I've decided to look in the mirror and love who is staring back at me
So walk away and take your hate with you
I'm still standing
I'm still here
I'm still me

Reality

I am the leaper you avoid and the truth you don't see
I am your reality
The first time I got to taste the fruit of his strength was when I saw him praying
To see a proud man's strong back arched toward Heaven is a picture painted in glory
Living life like he ought to
Like he was beholden to the One who came before him
Asking me to kneel beside him
I initially pulled away unfamiliar with genuine respect
You think I came here for pleasure
Pretty ain't pretty when pain shows up
Reality walked through my defenses, went deep inside my soul
Decrypting my scars as he whispered in my ear
Is the only way a man can love you, on his back
His machete cutting through grass never trimmed
I slowly exhaled as he convicted me with truth
Sowing pleasure and reaping it has made you empty
You say you are a child of He who you have not yet served
He is not an accomplice to your suffering

God has waited for you to recognize your greatness
But you are only content making more scars
Does it matter that God's got your back
When every man is invited in front
Pleasure has lived here long enough, I'm claiming you
But I will not feed your flesh
I am the answer to the questions you won't ask
I have watched you weaken, hoping you'd send for me
You only scream for pleasure
You are more concerned with the thread count of your Egyptian sheets than the man you got laying in them
Pleasure hoarding, trying to quench a thirst that sex can't heal
A man can't make you whole
He can't turn a pawn into a queen
Hearing truth made my ears bleed clarity
Now I'm grasping at God's straws
Trying to get meaning for my existence
Slowing reciting worth I have not yet built
Trying to break free from desire
Freedom is a state of mind that this Kizzie does not embrace

Living in this mind plantation

Whipping myself every time I consider leaving

Trying to taste freedom with slavery lips

Blurred lines surfacing in the mirror

In the thick of my own issues

Alone in my head I drift toward consciousness

Slowly releasing my tight grip

My hand gripping air

Looking for my conviction

No one present but me and my lust

Shattering my glass house I use pieces to cut Kizzie free

Breaking mental chains to sensual obsession

No angel or evil sit on my shoulders

Here slavery and freedom sit

Each waiting for my choice

Pick one Kizzie

Your thighs or your soul

Peace or be a piece

Dignity or dig on me

Pick one slave

Your soul is waiting

Duality

The duality that exists is real
Which side are you on
Why do you focus on the pebbles that have fallen
instead of the boulders that are still left
When a drop of purity descends from the Heavens
Do you see life descending or water spots
When your newborn expands their lungs
Do you observe their healthy, ability to cry or do you
hear screams of annoyance
When your friend reaches out for forgiveness
Do you appreciate their willingness to be humble or
do you let conceit fuel your cause
When problems infuse your life
Do you pray to God for guidance or do you shepherd
yourself to a resolution based on fear
When someone greets you with a genuine, caring,
affectionate smile
Are you grateful for their sincerity or focused on the
state of their teeth
When God saves you from everyday situations in life
Do you recognize His greatness and how blessed you
are or do you just say I was lucky

When unadulterated joy encompasses your heart, mind and soul
Do you bask deeply in it savoring every second or do you tell yourself you are not worthy of love
When someone tells you what they think of you do you make their words your own or do you examine the inner you for truth
If your life ended right now
Would you be more concerned with what people say about you at your funeral or where you were going to reside for eternity
When you look at yourself do you see an indomitable force that cannot be swayed or do you see someone that is easily lead
Are you more concerned with being called a Christian or living a life based on the Lord's Word
The duality that exists is real
Which side are you on

Not Jesus

I'm wrong but you can't see my intent
I'm sorry but you can't see my sorrow
I'm a liar but you can't see my truth
I'm not going to grovel in the dirt so you can look clean
I am a piece of black coal
Once thought to be insignificant
You only looked at me in my present state and thought I was disposable
You're so vain I bet you thought my pain was about you
Don't you, don't you
You judged me unworthy
You decided that I was unforgivable
You thought you could teach me
You thought you were so holy you were Jesus' substitute teacher
You say not me yet you sit on the judgement seat
You condemned me, without facts, with no regrets
You play Jesus but you can't handle that role
Jesus sacrificed, was willing to take punishment for things He didn't do

Blame is your middle name followed by somebody else
Everybody wants to be Christ until it's time to get on the cross
How many lashes could you take for another
How many thorns could press into your skull before you cried out, stop
Savior, you are not
Yet, it's easy for you to sit on your high chair and look down at my pain
Distant, unfeeling, motionless
You thought your obvious bias went unnoticed
Your joy at my pain
You could be one of His angels though
It's not the first time one went off the path
Hell's leader once sat high
He decided he'd rather live in the valley than on the mountain top
He has disciples too
Label me if you want
But Jesus you are not
The imitation is nothing like the original

You blame the devil for where you are but truth is you did all the work for him

He put the needle on the record but you listened to the whole album

The next time you say the devil made you do it

I'll ask you which one

The original, a disciple or you

Your counterfeit happiness is no mask for truth

You can't just listen to lyrics and it becomes true

You spent a lot of time humming it but I guess by now you realize Pharrell can't make you happy

Fake happiness

We need to be soul happy

That's what Christ offers

Genuine joy

Or would you rather sing the chorus of Happy instead

The Word

The Word lives
It stands and it speaks to all who hear it
The Bible says:
But my people are destroyed from a lack of knowledge
Slowly churning ignorance until its smooth like butter
When did we become so educated and yet so stupid
So smart, so focused on perfection
Grammar and annunciation looked upon as wisdom
I may not speak the King's English but I'm still a queen
Education is a great tool
But education does not make you Holy
We have become so driven on looking for faults that we no longer see good
Don't focus on flaws
I'm talking to you about life and living it more abundantly
I'm talking to you about spiritual awareness
I just gave you directions to your own salvation but you are so focused on my flaws you missed your exit to glory

We're so busy critiquing the messenger that we miss the message
Jesus is the Alpha and the Omega, the beginning and the end
Yet you think you can tell Him what's going to happen in the middle
Stop trying to "unqualify" people from roles that Jesus has already qualified them for
Remember Jesus does not use resumes
He didn't choose priests to be His disciples
He chose disciples and turned them into preachers
You have not because you ask not
No let me correct that, you don't "ask not",
you don't know what to ask for
Living in an apartment but praying for a Bugatti or Benz instead of a house
Childless but praying for a green eyed girl instead of a healthy child
"Manless" but praying for a 6' 2" piece of chiseled chocolate instead of a man who will love you as you stand
"Womanless" but praying for a six pack that can cook instead of a woman who will stand strong by your side

You have not because if you got what you asked for you'd be unhappier than you are right now

Don't ask God to fix your crutch unless you are willing to let it go

You hate it so much yet you use it everyday

You only need to lean on truth

God is that truth

Walk with God or stumble by yourself

Your crutch is your crutch

Praise

Let everything that has breath praise the Lord
But are you praising him or are you praising yourself
Basking in glory meant upward
We praise ourselves
Jesus is the light that takes away the sins of the world
Yet we act like we had something to do with His brilliance
When you got that job did you drop to your knees or pat yourself on the back
Did you thank the Lord or your interviewing skills
You can't praise God and yourself at the same time
Praise God
You should at least say thank you to the one who gave you the ability to speak
Every step you take has been guided by the Lord
But we're trying to look good
Fighting only for causes that make us seem giving
We are the ones have strayed off the path
We are the ones who disguise lies as truth
Let's look at the world we created:

1. There are 10 commandments but we act like they are just 10 suggestions

2. We can't name all of the disciples but we know the name of every member of the cast of Scandal
3. We sing about how we love Jesus while looking at someone we hate
4. We ask what would Jesus do but then we do what the devil would do
5. You say here I am use me Lord and as soon as He calls on you, you say why me
6. You go to a movie for 2 hours but if church runs 5 minutes late you're headed toward the door
7. You say the devil made you do it but you should really say you did it for the devil
8. Instead of making sure you wear the whole armor of God you're more focused on whether or not Sistah Mary is wearing a slip
9. You can quote what Cookie said on Empire but you can't quote what Christ said about salvation

10. We compare our blessings to other people but do not compare our burdens

We can't keep making excuses

Don't turn away from Christ

What God has perfected man has rejected

He has always loved us unconditionally

Isn't it time we loved Him the same way

Sin-cere

I'm losing weight so I wonder if I still need you
Your approval was my crutch
You were so comforting once but now I've outgrown you
I want to empty all of my trash at the same time
I thought you were real
Now I wonder if your reflection has ever been authentic
Quoting Scripture is how you got me
Not living it is why I'm leaving
My happier ever after started the day you left
Trying to find a Godly man
Instead I fell for a false prophet with a Biblical name
I made you into Goliath but I forgot I could be David
I was supposed to test the spirit
But the test was not supposed to be taken with my body
That was where I failed
I told myself the flesh is weak
No I was weak for giving into the flesh
I can't perfume flesh up, put it on a platter, light candles around it and then say the flesh is weak
No, the flesh was set up to fail

I can't fake understanding with orgasmic screams
Screaming does not dilute facts
Choices lead to pain
But I'm the one bleeding
I sliced myself trying to cut corners
I've gone deaf waiting to speak truth
I know I was original sin
I listened to a snake in a previous life
Now I'm on the eve of my awakening
No more Adams
The first man that broke my heart
Wrote his name into my book of lies
Now every man must pay for the ink of another
That's your 30 pieces of silver
Pay my price
Then kiss me on the cheek and get out

Here

Here's a cup of wisdom

Taken from your reflection

But this is not your first drop of your own self-worth

You get it

You are abundantly blessed with the knowledge that you are complete

You walk over liars

No reason to get dirty

You don't let fishermen hook you into being bait

So you relay your own parable

Give a man a fish he will eat for a night

Give a women a fish and she'll make 5 meals

Teach tell both to fish and they'll have their own business

Your vision is not limited by what you have now

You get up with a plan

Not a remote in your hand

You've seen it before

You can be so involved with The Walking Dead that you are The Living Walking

Walking to watch people who have already achieved their dreams

Social media is a great tool but more likes will never equal more love
More friends will never equal more business associates
And some people are content in mediocrity
You know you can't grow inundated by foolishness
You avoid crap and people call you snooty
If being a planner who is about our Father's business is snooty then make that your first and your last name
Names don't keep you from your destiny
Knowing that the sun shines does not get you any closer to walking in the light
Now people have to work harder to pull you out of your purpose
You are no longer willing sheep looking for their approval
You don't need an Amen from sheep
You got your Amen from God
Remember you can't explain to sheep what Kings and Queens do
So stop trying
We are not bigger than our calling

We are growing and we're looking for other folks who want to do more than talk about it, debate about it or post about it
We stumble, fall, get up, stumble fall, get up, stumble fall get up
Determination does not stop us for failing but it shows us we need to get up and try another way
What other people call failures we call attempts
When people say we have nothing we tell them I've lived with nothing and I kicked her out
When people say we started too late we tell them you can't win an endurance race with speed
Listen to that sound
As long as our heart beat continues so will we

 # Christian Truths

Some say I need to find God
Others say well you won't find Him at my church
If you cherish and worship the devil
Does it matter where you serve him
How can you be Christ like if you don't know who He is
Stop justifying sin by giving it titles
We try to make sin attractive
That is not your King
That is the one who uses his "scepter" on the Queen
If that's your King why don't you live in the same castle
You are not a mistress
Someone mistrusted you with their husband
If you are a King
Why do you spread your "seed" in several gardens
Sin is real
So practicing how to pronounce sin so its sounds seductive is wasting your time
Sin is universal
If sins were tattoos we'd all have some
We wouldn't be so quick to judge with our mistakes in plain sight

Judging is really minding my business without all the facts
Some of you are skipping toward hell and you stop to quote what I'm doing wrong
Sin ain't seasonal and hell is not a vacation spot
Don't be deceived by tell-lie-changing-vision (TV)
Sin is almost unrecognizable
It's packaged and enticing
You soon know more about shows than you do about your Bible
Sin is not in the background
It is hidden in plain sight
Focus
But don't focus on the sinner
Unless you want someone reading your scars
Remember sin is universal
And if sins were tattoos we'd all have some
So don't be so quick to read my tattoos
When I'm looking at all of yours

I'm Sorry

I'm sorry I moved to slow to stop you
Even though I saw you running toward the same cliff your momma jumped off
I'm sorry I thought I could stop you from going down the same path to hell that she took
But you only found places to walk where her footsteps had pressed the earth
I was not able to get you off of her path
I'm sorry that I saw your heart heading toward the floor and though I skid trying to prevent it from breaking I was unable to catch you
I'm sorry that I saw your pain but I couldn't prevent it from consuming you
You said you were fine but what you were really saying was you were fine suffering
I'm sorry that I couldn't prevent you from making the same mistakes as three generation of women with your last name
I was so determined to get you on a different path
I was so determined to make your life different
I was so determined to get you to hear God
But you were so determined to get down that path I couldn't stop you

I wish I was quicker

I wish I could run faster

I wish I stop you

But you're already over the cliff

I wish I could fly and save you

But even then I think you would glide into hell willingly

It's time I realized that I can't save you and you won't save you

So I just have to watch you self destruct

I'm sorry

I'll pray for you

I prayed for you

I cried for you

Forgive

Jesus said

I am not here to speak

I am here to listen

I focus on every breath you take

I know you

The real you

And I love everything about you

I see no flaws only humanity

I knew you would not be perfect

I knew you would make mistakes

Forgiveness is one of my gifts but you won't accept it

You turn away from it

I say you are lovable

I call you my child

I am here and I will always be here

I'll support you and strengthen you

I will never leave you

You may turn away from me

But every time you look back you will see Me standing here

Jesus thinks the world of you

Yet all you can think about is the world

God is a part of our entire life's journey

But so many of us pick Him up an drop Him off like he's a passenger

Forgive yourself

Stop punishing yourself for something that Jesus has already forgiven you for

Trust in the Lord

Believe what He says

Accept his love

Own your mistakes

Own your flaws

Now step into the light

No perfection is needed

Step into the light

Own who you are

Forgive yourself

Forgive yourself

Forgive yourself

Love

My husband kept me loved up
The backburner never did I see
He said the Trinity is first and my queen is second
Contentment complete
Until I allowed social "mediastic: thoughts to deter my path
So focused on the screen the lens near me were ignored
He asked me why does my queen want to become someone else's pawn
Loving things is not loving you
Let me talk to you about how real love feels
I can't even feel the presence of light when Jesus is not with me
He joined us together
All I need is a smile from your face and the once still world starts to revolve again
One drop of your sweat is like rainwater to my heart
Cleansing my palate your love encompasses me
He told me to inhale so he could get the rhythm of his heart back
His whispers alluring to my ears
I still hear his words breathing

I am not here to quench your thirst
But to make sure you never get thirsty in the first place
Sipping on his words made my heart full
His love echoes inside my heart
I can't imagine a world without my king
Love can't swim in the deep end of the pool with us
Even it's too shallow
We are one
He sets his heartbeat to mine
Our rhythm is in sync
When we stand even our shadows intermingle
This union is between two hearts
You can't stop what we have
You can't step in between us because there is no room
Even dreams dream of us
We are what love wants to be when it grows up
So simple, so real, untainted
Poison may flow from your lips but not into our relationship
We don't seek your input, approval, advice
We are just two married people in love

We know you don't see it often
But love is a gift we open every day
Praying the gift we left for each other is as glorious as the one we just received
We don't just lay down to love, we step up, get up and show up
Sade sang about it
1 Corinthians defined it
God embodies it
Love ain't ordinary
My husband sees that
I see that
Love won today
I'm so thankful
Love won today

Haiku

Goals
You can't use earthly
sources to reach eternal
goals. God got your plan.

Backup
You "sent" for me but
God answered the call. Why so
silent now huh? Click

The Way
God said He's the Way
so why do you insist on
getting in the way

My Pain
Strumming my pain with
his fingers but Jesus moved
his hand out the way

Answer
The Lord listens
to your prayers but do you hear
His answers or yours

Fall
How many times do
you have to fall before you
stop tripping yourself

Two Masters
You work for satan
while trying to serve Jesus,
two masters, one fool.

Worship
You won't spend time to
worship Him but you want Him
to solve your problems

Love
Your love is only
puddle deep and this ocean
won't deal with puddles

Beginning
In the beginning
God created man and then
we created doubt

Chase
Queens don't chase Kings and
Kings don't chase Queens. If you want
a mate act like one

Job
Companionship is
not a solution to pain.
Don't give love a job

Broken
Look your mirror is
not broken, you are. Pieces
of truth can't fix lies

Love Can't
Love can't conquer hate.
Without conviction and faith
love is just a word

Stop
Let me be clear Christ
will never send you to be
with someone else's spouse

Shelf
If you think you can
put Jesus on a shelf, you
don't know who you serve

Burnt Churches
Burning down churches
you know the owner sees you.
Think, this is God's house

False
Stop listening to
false prophets. Your soul's sick of
their brand of poison

Prayer
Walking with Jesus
it's a road worth traveling
bend down start today

Men
Strong men don't need you
to make them relevant. God
already did that.

Kimism

Kimism

A multifaceted God did not create one dimensional people.

You have more than one talent.

Do you know all of them... OR are you putting one blessing on the table and pretending it's full?

Kimism

If someone hurts you and your first thought is plotting how to get back at them...

Aren't you about to do the very thing you just complained about?

Kimism

Stop giving Satan credit

for your work

Notes